The British Museum

THE PLOT AGAINST THE EMPEROR

AN ANCIENT ROMAN PUZZLE MYSTERY

ANDY SEED

JAMES WESTON LEWIS

To everyone at Bessacarr Primary School, with very best wishes – A.S.

For Mabli Clem, with all my love – J.W.L.

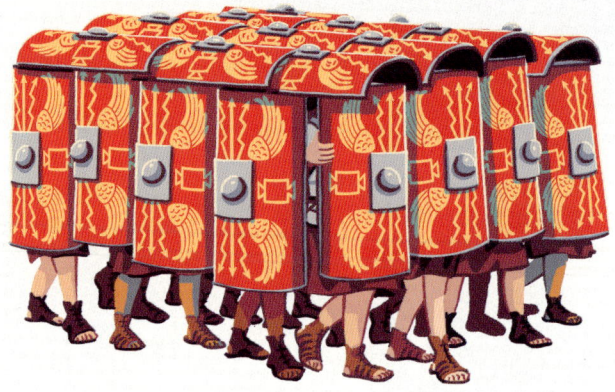

First published 2023 by Nosy Crow Ltd
Wheat Wharf, 27a Shad Thames,
London, SE1 2XZ, UK

Nosy Crow Eireann Ltd
44 Orchard Grove, Kenmare,
Co Kerry, V93 FY22, Ireland

www.nosycrow.com

ISBN 978 1 83994 708 7 (HB)
ISBN 978 1 83994 645 5 (PB)

Nosy Crow and associated logos are trademarks and/or registered trademarks of Nosy Crow Ltd.

Published in collaboration with the British Museum.

Text © Andy Seed 2023
Illustrations © James Weston Lewis 2023

The right of Andy Seed to be identified as the author and James Weston Lewis to be identified as the illustrator of this work has been asserted.

All rights reserved.

This book is sold subject to the condition that it shall not, by way of trade or otherwise, be lent, hired out or otherwise circulated in any form of binding or cover other than that in which it is published. No part of this publication may be reproduced, stored in a retrieval system, or transmitted in any form or by any means (electronic, mechanical, photocopying, recording or otherwise) without the prior written permission of Nosy Crow Ltd.

A CIP catalogue record for this book is available from the British Library.

Printed in China.
Papers used by Nosy Crow are made from wood grown in sustainable forests.

1 3 5 7 9 8 6 4 2 (HB)
1 3 5 7 9 8 6 4 2 (PB)

CONTENTS

Introduction	4	IV
Plotters in the Forum	6	VI
Hiding in the Pantheon	10	X
The Search at the Aqueduct	14	XIV
Danger at the Campus Martius	16	XVI
Shoe Trouble	20	XX
Bathtime	24	XXIV
Clue at the Colosseum	26	XXVI
A Deadly Cargo	30	XXX
A Race at the Circus Maximus	34	XXXIV
Voices at the Victory Parade	38	XXXVIII
A Deadly Banquet	40	XL
Guilty!	44	XLIV
Puzzle Solutions	46	XLVI
Glossary	48	XLVIII

INTRODUCTION

Welcome to ancient Rome, the greatest city on Earth. It is the 1st Century AD and something shocking is about to happen. Can you help young Roman friends Flavia and Julius escape from disaster and save the emperor?

JULIUS

Julius is the son of a tribune, an army officer who is in charge of a cohort of 500 Roman soldiers. He lives in a villa on the edge of Rome and loves learning about the history of the mighty Roman Empire. Julius has already learned how to write in Latin and he enjoys making notes as he explores the great city with his friend Flavia.

FLAVIA

Flavia is the daughter of the senior aquarius, who is in charge of the huge stone aqueducts that supply water to the city of Rome. She is sporty and daring, always on the lookout for adventure, although she is expected to help around the house more than she would like. Flavia is learning Latin with a tutor at home but would rather be outdoors having fun.

CODEBREAKER

Flavia and Julius are in a race against time to stop a group of Roman villains from carrying out a dreadful plan. On their adventure they have to solve a series of puzzles, but can you help them? The people of ancient Rome spoke in a language called Latin, which this book will help you to read. It's like cracking a code. Follow the clues on each page and use the special charts and dictionary at the back of the book to help you unravel the secrets of the Roman plotters!

Here's an example:

PUZZLE
What are these two Roman soldiers saying?

estne scutum novum?

sic

The first soldier is asking a question. Looking in the guide at the back of the book, you can see what it means:

LATIN PHRASES

| est puella et puer: The girl and the boy |
| estne scutum novum?: Is that a new shield? |
| estne coclea?: Is that the snail? |

LATIN WORDS

sandalia	shoes
senator	senator
sic	yes

↓

The first soldier is saying,
'Is that a new shield?'

↓

The second soldier
is saying, 'yes'

OBSERVATION CHALLENGE

Rome was a place full of rats as well as people. Can you spot a rat in each scene? The wolf is the symbol of the city. Can you find three wolves hidden in the book, too?

PLOTTERS IN THE FORUM

"Race you to the top of the Capitoline Hill!" called Flavia, dashing up the stone steps.

"There's no point," said Julius, panting. "You always win. Anyway, I want to show you something special over there."

They walked across the south side of the hill to a craggy area covered in bushes. Julius pointed to the long drop below them. "This is the Tarpeian Rock. My dad said that the authorities used to throw criminals off here."

Flavia was about to reply when she heard voices behind them. Peering through the undergrowth, the children saw two well-dressed men and a woman, speaking in hushed tones. As they listened, Julius's face turned red and Flavia gulped. It was clear these people were planning something dreadful.

DID YOU KNOW?

Rome was the biggest city in the ancient world and home to over one million people! At its centre was the Forum, a large public square which acted as a meeting place and somewhere to hold special events. It was surrounded by important government buildings, temples and monuments.

The three figures were looking at something. The woman crouched down and pushed it under a rock while two large men kept a lookout. As they walked away towards the Forum, Flavia scurried out and pulled the object from its hiding place. It was a lead tablet with words scratched into the surface.

She had almost made it back to where Julius was hiding when they heard a shout. The people were coming back! "They've seen us!" Julian yelped. "We've got to run, come on!"

"After them!" the woman ordered to the two henchmen at her side.

PUZZLE

What does the message on the lead tablet say? It is written in Latin, the language spoken by the ancient Romans, but some of the letters were rubbed away by the rock when Flavia picked it up. To help you crack the code, use the guide at the back of the book.

CODE CLUE

The Romans used nearly all of the letters we use today. The Latin alphabet had 21 letters (J, U, W, Y and Z were not used at this time).

HIDING IN THE PANTHEON

"They can't really be planning to kill the emperor, can they?" said Flavia, as they reached a busy road and hid in a doorway. "Especially when he's just won that big battle in Dacia and everyone in the city is celebrating."

"My father told me that rivals are always trying to overthrow Rome's leaders and seize power," said Julius. "We need to tell someone urgently!"

As they stepped on to the street, Flavia saw the two henchmen who had been ordered to find them. "Hurry, we can hide from them in the Pantheon!"

THE SEARCH AT THE AQUEDUCT

"Thank the gods!" sighed Flavia, as the two henchmen left the Pantheon.

"This is serious," said Julius. "We've got to get help."

Flavia nodded. "My father will be at one of the aqueducts. Come on, let's run!"

They dashed across the crowded city to the northern district, where a great arched bridge of stone brought fresh water into Rome. The two friends searched the site but could not find the aquarius, Flavia's father.

"Excuse me," Flavia asked an overseer who was helping some men to replace part of the walls. "Do you know where the aquarius is?"

"He'll be at whichever aqueduct needs the most repairs," muttered the dusty foreman. "And this afternoon he's due at the baths."

Julius groaned. "How will we know which aqueduct that is?"

The man fetched a scroll covered in writing. "It says here how many new blocks of stone each one needs."

AQUAEDUCTUS	LAPIDES
AQUA APPIA	LXXII
AQUA MARCIA	CCCXXVIII
AQUA ANIO VETUS	XV
AQUA CLAUDIA	CDXVI
AQUA TEPULA	CLXVII
AQUA JULIA	VIII
AQUA VIRGO	LIX
AQUA ALSIETINA	CDXIV
AQUA ANIO NOVUS	CCXXIX

The two friends hurried across Rome to the huge Campus Martius, where the army training took place. As they ran along the busy cobbled streets, they passed stray dogs and stalls filled with bright spices and pungent cheeses.

"Oh no!" Julius said, as he slipped. "My sandal strap has broken!"

"There's no time to stop now!" shouted Flavia.

When they arrived, the place was heaving with soldiers and people watching the special training routines. Officers barked out orders above the sound of stomping feet and swords clattering against shields.

"My father will be around here somewhere," said Julius. "His helmet has a black crest."

"Is that him over there?" said Flavia.

"Yes!" said Julius. "But we can't go up to him now!"

PUZZLES

1. Why can't the two friends go straight over to Julius's father?
2. Flavia thinks that the army may be involved in the plot against the emperor. What has she noticed?

DID YOU KNOW?

The Campus Martius was a large area of Rome where army training took place. If a Roman citizen wanted to become a well-paid legionary soldier, he had to sign up for 25 years of service! He would have to stay fit and learn many skills, including how to use weapons such as a sword, javelin, bow and arrow or a large catapult.

SHOE TROUBLE

"I can't believe that crooked senator persuaded some of the army to help with the plot against the emperor!" Flavia fumed.

"I just hope my father isn't involved," said Julius, but before they could reach him, they heard a shout. One of the henchmen had spotted them!

"Run!" said Julius.

"We'll never shake off these brutes," panted Flavia. "They're still chasing us!"

"And my sandals are falling apart," Julius said, tripping over a paving stone. "What shall we do?"

"Quick, into that shoe shop!" said Flavia, darting through a doorway in one of the insulae. Julius followed, before the henchmen spotted them.

"What have you got in your purse?" asked Flavia, as she inspected a pair of sandals.

"Erm, two coins, a broken stylus, half a hairy fig and lots of dust," said Julius.

Flavia rolled her eyes. "Well, I suppose I will have to use the money I was saving up for a necklace."

"I'll pay you back," said Julius. "And it'll be worth it if we can save the emperor."

PUZZLE
Which is the only pair of sandals that the children can buy?

 CODE CLUE

Here are some of the coins used in ancient Rome:

As: a small copper coin like a penny, worth a value of 1 as

Sestertius: a brass coin worth a value of 4 asses

Denarius: a silver coin worth 16 asses

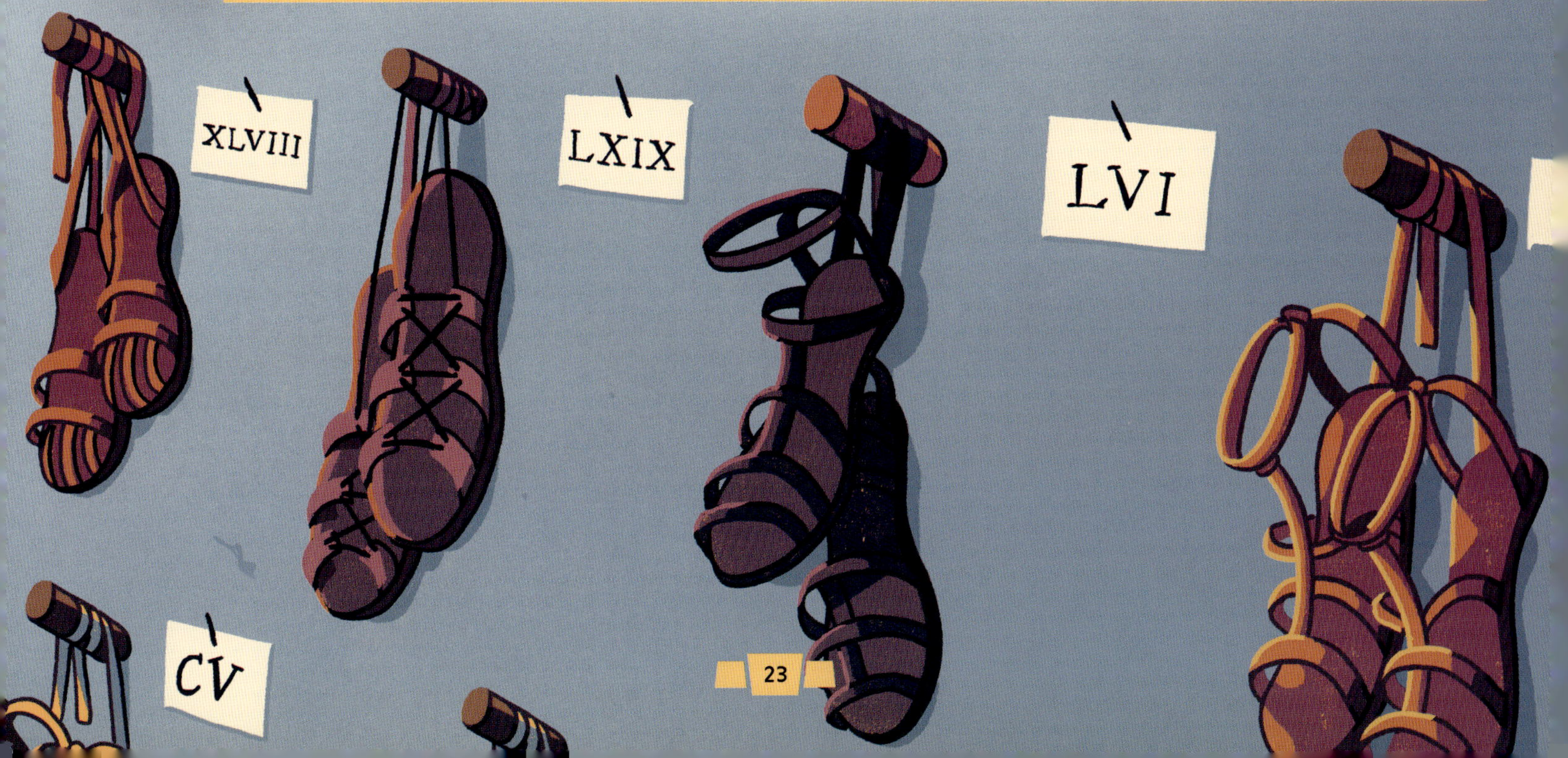

CIV

XLVIII

LXIX

LVI

CV

BATHTIME

"That's much better!" said Julius. "But what are we going to do now?"

Flavia stopped, deep in thought. "We're right by the baths!"

Julius screwed up his face. "The emperor's life is in peril and you want to have a wash?"

"No, silly, I mean my father might be there. The overseer at the aqueduct said he was due here this afternoon. Come on."

DID YOU KNOW?

The Romans loved their public baths. They were places for people to meet, wash, swim and exercise (like a modern-day gym). There were hot baths, warm baths and cold baths. People didn't bathe on their own, it was an activity they did with others.

DID YOU KNOW?

The Colosseum was a giant building, as big as a large football stadium, which held over 50,000 people. Romans came to watch all kind of events there, including gladiator contests, executions, fights between large wild animals and recreations of famous battles. Most gladiators were specially trained slaves, criminals or prisoners.

donum speciale ad Ostiam advenit

CLUE AT THE COLOSSEUM

"This is hopeless," said Julius, as they ran out on to the busy street. "There are plotters everywhere."

"We mustn't give up," said Flavia. "Perhaps we need to warn the emperor himself."

"You're right – but where will he be? There are celebrations in his honour all over the city!"

"What about the Colosseum? I heard there are special events there with the empire's greatest gladiators. He might be watching. Come on!" Flavia started moving before Julius could reply.

Soon, the two friends stood inside the immense amphitheatre. Rowdy crowds shouted and cheered as two sweaty gladiators fought in the arena.

"Look," said Julius. "It's that woman we saw on the Capitoline Hill!" She was talking to a tall man. The two children crept closer to hear what she was saying . . .

PUZZLE
The woman said something has arrived at Ostia. What is it?

Flavia's eyes grew wide. "We must get to the port of Ostia," she cried. "It could be an important clue!"

But she had been too loud. The woman turned around and gave a frown. "Get hold of those two now!" she ordered to the henchmen, who had just burst into the crowd.

Flavia and Julius scampered down the nearest steps and frantically looked for a way out of the Colosseum. There were many doorways, but the signs were missing.

"Which one is the exit?" cried Julius.

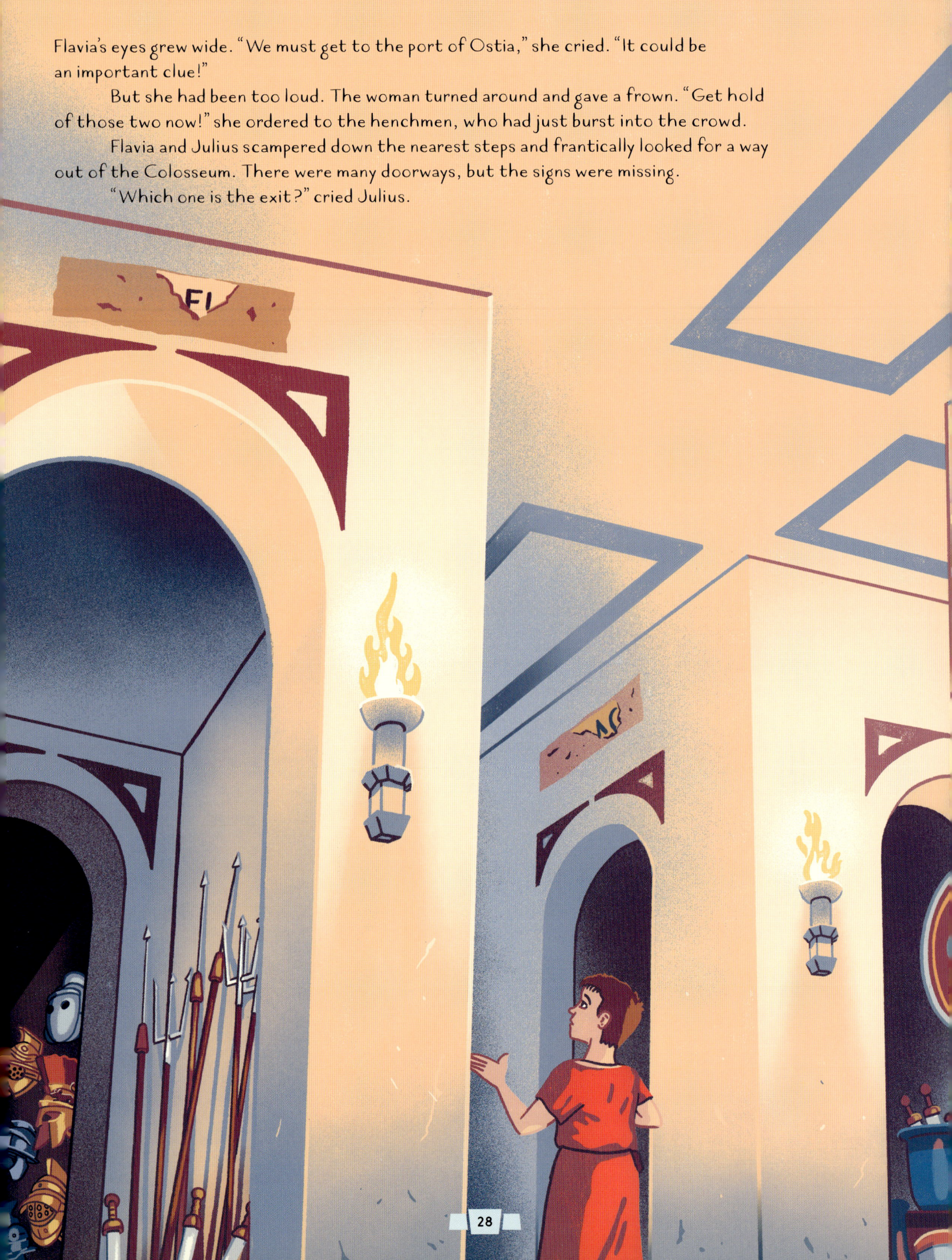

PUZZLE

Flavia and Julius have spotted pieces of a broken clay tile on the floor. It looks like an exit sign. Are they right? And which door does it belong to? It will help to trace the pieces on paper and cut them out.

A DEADLY CARGO

Julius and Flavia managed to catch a bumpy ride on a horse and cart going to Ostia. After a few hours they arrived at the busy coastal port which served the great city of Rome. The harbour was a scene of endless activity with ships and boats arriving and leaving, cargo being loaded and unloaded, and people, horses and carts everywhere. Men were shouting and there was a strong smell of fish in the air.

"This place really stinks!" said Flavia.

"Never mind that," said Julius. "We need to discover the special gift that the plotters were talking about."

DID YOU KNOW?

Ostia was a port 25 kilometres from Rome. Here, ships and boats from all over the empire landed with cargoes of grain, other foods and all kinds of products. These were then taken by barge along the River Tiber to the city.

At that moment, a long troopship pulled into the docks. It was crowded with soldiers, who began to come ashore as soon as the vessel was tied up. Five more empty military ships could be seen along one of the piers.

"Wait a minute," said Julius. "These soldiers are not supposed to be here! My father told me this legion is stationed in Gaul until May."

"We must go and find the emperor!" said Flavia.

A RACE AT THE CIRCUS MAXIMUS

After a bumpy lift on another cart, Julius and Flavia finally arrived at the Circus Maximus, the gigantic stadium with its long racetrack and spectacular banks of spectators. Great cheers went up for the chariot riders hurtling along through clouds of dust.

"Where's the emperor?" said Flavia, scanning the endless crowds.

"He's right over there, in his place of honour," said Julius. "It'll take us ages to reach him."

"But look who else is here," Flavia gasped. "And much nearer!" They watched as the tall plotter passed something to the senator, and the senator gave the tall man a scroll in return.

DID YOU KNOW?

The Circus Maximus was Rome's biggest arena, a giant 600-metre-long track used for all kinds of races, games, parades and public events. Even wild animal hunts were staged there. There was room for about 250,000 spectators, three times more than can fit in a modern Olympic stadium!

The two friends crept nearer to the plotters to see what they were doing.

"We have to get that scroll. The emperor's life is in danger!" whispered Flavia.

Before Julius could try and stop her, Flavia darted forward and snatched at the document.

"Hey!" one of the henchmen shouted, as a piece of the papyrus tore away.

Flavia and Julius fled down the steps through the spectators, chased by the two henchmen and the tall stranger. The friends ducked down and crawled among the legs of the noisy crowd. Once out of the stadium, they found a quiet corner to read the torn fragment of the scroll.

VOICES AT THE VICTORY PARADE

"The emperor's brother!" the children gasped! They knew they had to act fast. By now the emperor would be on a victory parade through the streets, celebrating his military triumph. They joined the waiting crowds along the route and climbed on to a low wall.

"We might be able to call out and warn him from here as he passes," said Flavia.

"But what shall we say?" said Julius. "There are so many people involved in this plot."

"Yeah, 'don't eat anything at your feast' is going to sound weird." Julius took out his wax tablet and stylus. "I'll write down some ideas."

"Hurry up," said Flavia. "The parade is nearly here!"

Julius and Flavia shouted and waved their messages wildly but it was no use – the emperor couldn't see them in the crowd.

"We'll have to go to the palace," sighed Flavia. "It's our only chance."

PUZZLE

Julius wrote down some words, but didn't have time to put them in order. Can you work out what his message was going to be?

The words are:
MORTIFERUS, VENIUNT, ET, CIBUS, MILITES

A DEADLY BANQUET

The friends dashed up to the door of the Imperial Palace, where two large guards stood blocking the entrance.

"Let us in! The emperor is in terrible danger!" said Julius. "We need to speak to him now."

"Go away, you silly brats," growled one of the men. "You're talking nonsense."

"OK then, what's this?" said Flavia, holding up the lead tablet. As the guard looked at it, the two friends dashed past him to the banquet hall.

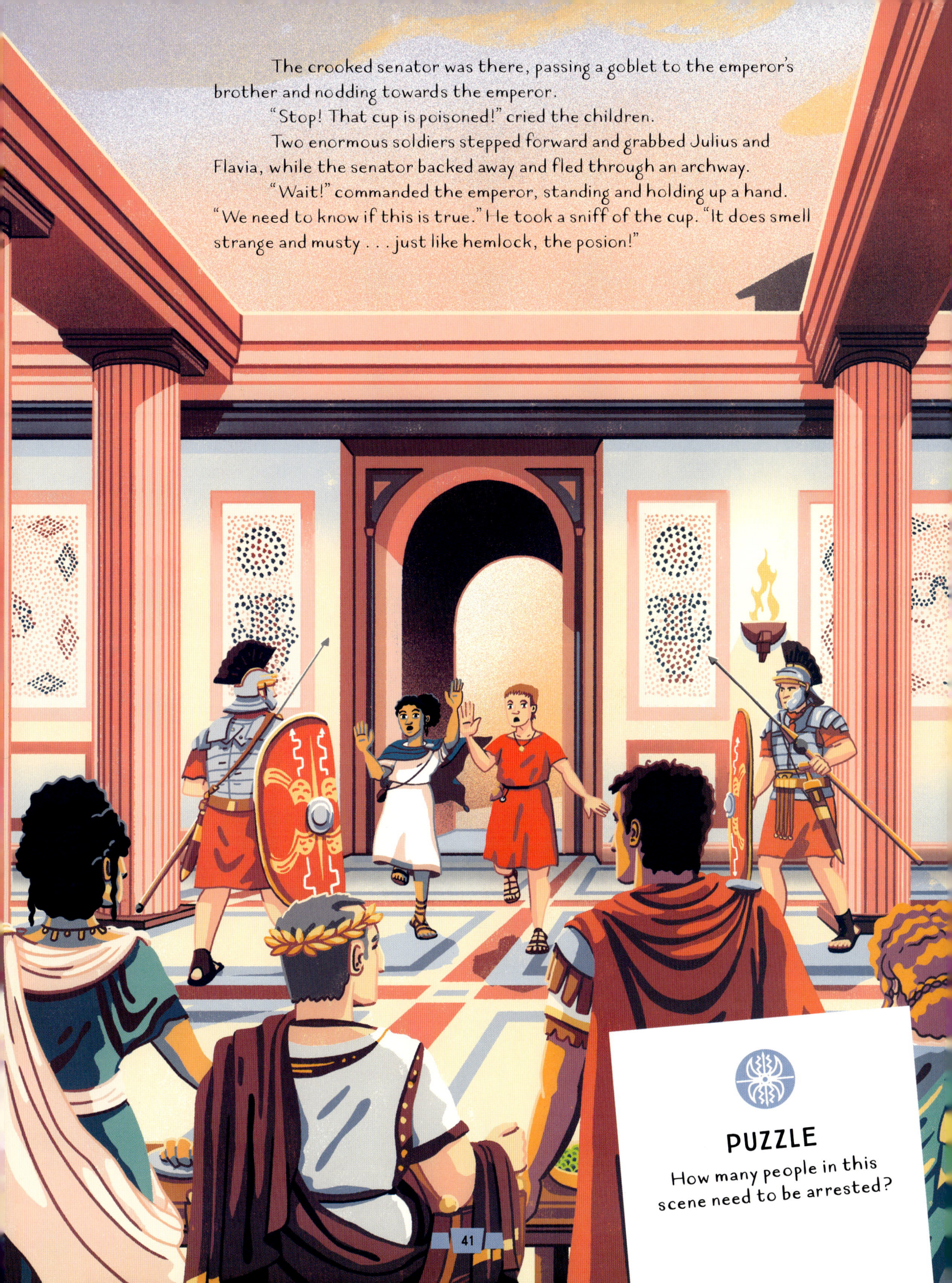

The crooked senator was there, passing a goblet to the emperor's brother and nodding towards the emperor.

"Stop! That cup is poisoned!" cried the children.

Two enormous soldiers stepped forward and grabbed Julius and Flavia, while the senator backed away and fled through an archway.

"Wait!" commanded the emperor, standing and holding up a hand. "We need to know if this is true." He took a sniff of the cup. "It does smell strange and musty . . . just like hemlock, the posion!"

PUZZLE
How many people in this scene need to be arrested?

At last, the children had a chance to explain everything they had seen and heard during the day.

"So, some of my soldiers are involved in this vile plot too?" said the emperor.

"Yes, the Eighth Legion has landed at Ostia! We saw them," said Flavia.

"We must send a rider there immediately," commanded the emperor. "Any soldier marching on Rome will be guilty of treason!" He turned and glared at his brother, who hung his head in shame. "And my own brother was behind this too. You always wanted to rule in my place, you traitor!"

"But where is the wicked senator who was passing him the poison?" said Julius. "He's the real leader of this plot."

"Well, who is he?" rumbled the emperor.

"I don't know his name," said Flavia, "but he was sitting over there with a plate of strawberries when he passed the cup."

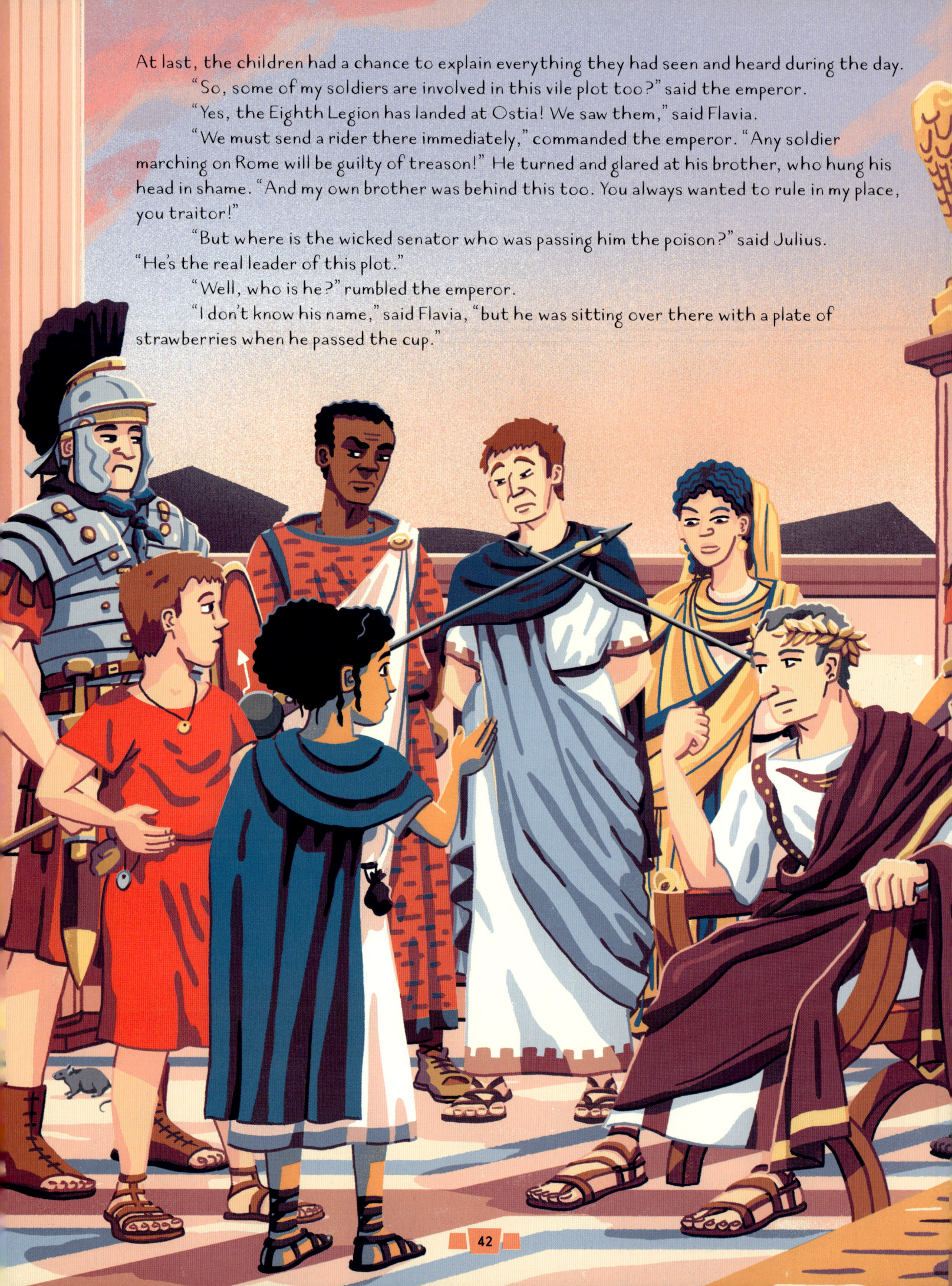

PUZZLE

Can you help the children work out the senator's name from what the servant tells them?

CODE CLUE

There were four bowls of fruit at that table: uvae, persicae, fraga and cerasi.

"My servant, Philus, might be able to help," said the emperor. "He knows exactly what the senators like to eat."

At this, Philus stepped forward. "Varro only eats green foods," he said. "And Quintus likes fruit in bunches. Magnus won't eat anything with a stone in it. As for Rufus, he prefers large fruit."

"I think I know who it was," said Julius.

GUILTY!

Just a short time later, the guilty senator, Magnus, was brought before the emperor by two hulking soldiers. The emperor stared at him with fury. "Well, what have you to say, senator?"

Magnus cleared his throat. "I was here at the banquet earlier, of course. I wanted to celebrate your magnificent victory. But all of the other senators were here too. These foolish children have clearly mistaken me for another man."

"But we can prove it," said Flavia.

PUZZLE
What was the children's final piece of evidence? Looking back through the book, can you find one key item that proves Magnus was part of the plot?

CODE CLUE
It is a piece of something larger.

When the children had finished explaining their evidence to the emperor, he gave a broad smile. "Astonishing! It has taken two children to save my life and prevent the overthrow of a mighty empire. I will make sure that you are given a great reward. Let's start with some of this banquet food!"

PUZZLE SOLUTIONS

PAGE 9 – PLOTTERS IN THE FORUM
The Roman words on the lead tablet are **today**, **poison**, **emperor**.

PAGE 13 – HIDING IN THE PANTHEON
The children should hide behind **Minerva** because she has a weapon and is the goddess of wisdom.

The baddies are saying "We will find those children soon" and "The others are searching too."

PAGE 14 – THE SEARCH AT THE AQUEDUCT
The correct aqueduct is **Aqua Claudia**, which needs **416 stones**.

PAGE 19 – DANGER AT THE CAMPUS MARTIUS
1. The reason is that the children's two pursuers and a plotter are there in the crowd, between them and Julius's father.

2. The reason is that one of the plotters (the bad senator) is in the crowd talking to a senior army commander about the plan.

PAGE 21 – SHOE TROUBLE
1. The one that says 'SANDALIA' (which means **shoes**) above the door.

2. Several people in the scene are talking via speech bubbles. One of them is saying, 'est puella et puer' (which means 'It's a girl and a boy') – this is the lookout.

PAGE 23 – SHOE TROUBLE
Julius has **1 as** and **1 sestertius**. Flavia has **2 sestertius** and **2 denarius**. This added up to **45 asses**. They can afford the sandals that cost XLV.

PAGE 25 – BATHTIME
1. Here is the safe route through the baths:

2. The person who has been to Spain is circled in blue.

   The person who wants a new towel is circled in yellow.

   The person who is gathering swords is circled in pink.

PAGE 27 – CLUE AT THE COLOSSEUM
The special gift has arrived in Ostia

PAGE 29 - CLUE AT THE COLOSSEUM
The word on the tile says OSTIUM which means **exit**.

The correct door is circled below:

PAGE 33 - A DEADLY CARGO
1. The special gift is **soldiers**.
2. The villainous senator is seen speaking to a centurion or other officer.
3. VIII, the **Eighth Legion**.
4. **Friday** and **March** as mentioned in speech bubbles.
5. The two workers say that the emperor will be at the **Circus Maximus**.

PAGE 37 - A RACE AT THE CIRCUS MAXIMUS
The crime is due to happen at the **banquet**, and the emperor's **brother** is involved.

PAGE 39 - VOICES AT THE VICTORY PARADE
The words are **deadly**, **come**, **and**, **food**, **soldiers**. Possible answers are 'soldiers come and deadly food' or 'soldiers and deadly food come' or 'deadly food and soldiers come'.

PAGE 41 - A DEADLY BANQUET
Four people need to be arrested: the **senator**, the **emperor's brother**, the **tall plotter** and the **woman** next to him in yellow.

PAGE 43 - A DEADLY BANQUET
The answer is **Magnus**:

uvae means **grapes**
persicae means **peaches**
fraga means **strawberries**
cerasi means **cherries**

Varro only eats green food so he could only have eaten the grapes.

Quintus only eats fruit in bunches so he could only have eaten the grapes or the cherries.

Rufus prefers large fruit so he could only have eaten the peaches.

Therefore, Magnus is the only one who could have eaten the strawberries.

PAGE 45 - GUILTY!
The parchment fragment that the children found on page 37 had the initial **M** on it, which stood for **Magnus**.

The three wolves are on pages **9**, **17** and **40**.

GLOSSARY

Amphitheatre An open circular or oval building with seats surrounding a central space used for large events

Aquarius The Roman official in charge of the large stone aqueducts which brought water into cities and towns

Aqueduct A type of bridge or channel used to carry water

Authorities The people in charge of something important like a town

Banquet A large feast shared by many people to celebrate something

Campus Martius The 'Field of Mars' was a large open space where the Roman army trained, and was also used for voting and for festivals

Cargo Things or goods carried by a boat or a wheeled vehicle

Chariot A horse-drawn vehicle used for racing or warfare

Citizen A Roman person who was protected by laws and had the right to vote, own property, become an official and do many other things

Colosseum The giant amphitheatre in Rome where many events were held, such as gladiator fights and recreated battles

Emperor The powerful ruler of the Roman Empire

Gaul A large area of the Roman Empire, roughly where France is located today

Gladiator A person (often an enslaved person or criminal) who would fight to the death for the entertainment of the Roman public

Insulae Roman buildings similar to blocks of flats which housed people and sometimes included shops on the ground floor

Javelin A type of spear for throwing, carried by Roman soldiers

Legion An army division of about 5,000 soldiers

Legionary A soldier who was grouped with other soldiers into a legion

Ostia A port town about 25 kilometres from Rome

Pantheon An impressive building in Rome first used as a temple for worshipping Roman gods and goddesses

Papyrus Paper-like material made from reed stems

Senator An important person who was a member of the Senate, a group of leaders which helped govern the Roman Empire

Stylus A short, pointed stick used to write on a wax tablet or other surface

Tablet A flat piece of wood covered in a thin layer of wax, used for writing on

Testudo Latin for 'tortoise', and a form of defence in which an advancing group of soldiers used their shields to surround themselves with a protective shell

Treason The extremely serious crime committed when a person tries to kill or betray the leader of their own country, or take it over themselves

Triumph A victory parade for a commander or emperor who had achieved an important military success

Tribune A commander in the Roman army